19.95

VOICEPLAY

22 Songs for Young Children

compiled and written by
Alison Street and Linda Bance

series editor: Peter Hunt

MUSIC DEPARTMENT

OXFORD

UNIVERSITY PRESS

OXFORD
UNIVERSITY PRESS

Great Clarendon Street, Oxford OX2 6DP, England
198 Madison Avenue, New York, NY10016, USA

Oxford University Press is a department of the University of Oxford.
It furthers the University's aim of excellence in research, scholarship,
and education by publishing worldwide in

Oxford   New York
Auckland   Cape Town   Hong Kong   Karachi
Kuala Lumpur   Madrid   Melbourne   Mexico City   Nairobi
New Delhi   Shanghai   Taipei   Toronto

With offices in

Argentina   Austria   Brazil   Chile   Czech Republic   France   Greece
Guatemala   Hungary   Italy   Japan   Poland   Portugal   Singapore
South Korea   Switzerland   Thailand   Turkey   Ukraine   Vietnam

Oxford is a registered trade mark of Oxford University Press
in the UK and in certain other countries

Music and text origination by
Barnes Music Engraving Ltd., East Sussex
Printed in Great Britain on acid-free paper by
Caligraving Limited, Thetford, Norfolk

Cover illustration by Laure Fournier.
Icons by Philip Atkins.
Illustrations on p. 11 by John Grandidge.

Foreword

Children sing as part of everyday life, easily and unselfconsciously. Singing is not complicated, nor special, nor something they have anxieties about. They play with songs and sing as they play. They sing made-up tunes and bits of songs they have remembered from family, from television, or from favourite CDs.

However, alongside this everyday ease with singing, children should also have the chance to learn and practise singing skills. This learning can be woven into the playing, the moving, the activities, and stories in which children intuitively engage when singing. The challenge is to find a good balance between playing with songs and the focus and concentration involved in learning to become a singer.

Voiceplay achieves that balance. It offers good songs, ideas, and guidance. It now waits only for the children, parents, and practitioners who will sing its songs into life.

SUSAN YOUNG

Series Editor's Note

It gives me enormous pleasure to introduce *Voiceplay*. Singing is a natural activity for young children, and one in which they engage with energy and enthusiasm. With encouragement and guidance, it becomes a gift which not only brings pleasure to young people and their communities, but also contributes to all aspects of children's lives and personal development.

Children learn to listen, to share, to be creative, and to respect others by taking part in well-organized group activities. Through singing and making music at a young age, they acquire a good sense of pitch and pulse, and learn how to use their voices expressively and confidently. These musical and social skills form a foundation for life-long learning.

It is for all of these reasons that *Voiceplay* is a very welcome addition to the *Voiceworks* series. For use by all practitioners in any Early Years setting, the songs and activities are attractive and very accessible, and the supporting notes will help any leader achieve success, getting the best out of both the material and the children!

Alison Street and Linda Bance are superbly qualified for the task of bringing the excitement of singing to life for young children. Between them they have a huge range of practical experience which has been carefully applied to produce an outstanding collection of songs and activities. This is a wonderfully inspired book that will empower all who use it to go on singing and learning. Good luck and happy singing!

PETER HUNT

Contents

Introduction

▨ Who is this book for?

This songbook is for practitioners working in Early Years settings and also for parents and carers at home. Whether you are running a session with thirty children or sitting in a corner with three, *Voiceplay* shows you how you can use your voice to lead others and help young children develop their singing.

▨ Using Voiceplay

Musical terms

The following terms are used in this book:

- **Pitch**   the way tunes move up and down; high sounds and low sounds
- **Beat**   the steady pulse underlying the music
- **Rhythm**   the long and short sounds and silences in sequence
- **Timbre**   the quality of the sound
- **Dynamics**   how loud or quiet the sound is
- **Phrase**   a musical sentence

Choosing the songs

Whether you are indoors or outside, with children for ten minutes or half an hour, this book helps you make the most of the time you have together by providing songs for different situations. Most of the songs are very flexible and can be adapted as required, but they have been divided into five broad categories to help guide you. The songs are given in progressive order within each section.

- **Section 1: Songs to help things happen**
  These help with daily routines, like gathering people together.

- **Section 2: Songs with movement**
  These are particularly suitable if you are planning a movement activity. They encourage children to use movement and to sing while moving.

- **Section 3: Songs to help singing voices**
  These help develop children's singing voices by using short phrases, echoes, and pitch matching.

- **Section 4: Songs for play**
  These explore links with how children like to play. They can be adapted to fit any activity the children are doing, be it moulding play-dough or pushing a toy truck.

- **Section 5: Songs that tell stories**
  These tell familiar stories and allow children to tell their own. They also encourage more focused group singing.

Singing the songs

The songs are presented with clear instructions to help guide you through leading and teaching them. The layout for each is identical:

- **Choose this song** sets out the reasons for using a particular song.

- **Get ready** explains what you need to think about before you start singing, like whether the children should be sitting or standing.

- **Sing this song** is about ways of teaching and singing through the song.

- **Ideas** are for making the most of a song and can include musical, movement, and play activities.

The music for all songs includes basic chord symbols for guitar or keyboard. Four songs have written-out piano accompaniments which are given on pp. 62–3. These are: 'Barney Bear', 'Seer moonday goday paer (Head and shoulders)', 'I live in the city', and 'The wolf's tale'. With the exception of 'The wolf's tale', the accompaniments may be photocopied.

The CD

The CD contains all of the songs, many with instrumental accompaniments. If you're unsure how to read music, you can learn the songs solely by listening to them. The CD shows how to lead the children in singing by using 'Ready, let's go' (see 'Singing with young children', p. 8). It also provides examples of many of the extension activities given in the 'Ideas' sections. Each song is headed with the relevant CD track number.

Voice play

If possible, it's a good idea to help children prepare for singing by encouraging them to play around with their voices. The next section, 'Voice play', suggests breathing activities and voice sounds to help you do this; examples are given on the CD. This section also includes a song, 'Copy kitten', which helps to develop voice play ideas.

The children's book

The illustrated children's book in your leader's pack includes pictures and words for 11 of the songs. It provides an additional resource that can be used during singing sessions to aid children's understanding of song ideas and activities and stimulate creative development. It can also be added to music and literacy corners to encourage children to engage independently with the songs and their words. Information on which songs are included in the children's book is given at the top of the relevant songs in the leader's book. Additional copies of the children's book (ISBN 978–0–19–321061–5) may be purchased separately.

Voice sounds, singing, and movement

Voice sounds and movement are usually closely linked for young children. They often make sounds when bouncing, crouching, or spinning around, and these can be both 'involuntary' responses to movement and give meaning to words which describe movement. Many of the songs in this book include actions and movement activities which build upon this link to encourage children to use their voices expressively.

For further information on using singing and movement activities with young children, please see the reading list on p. 64.

Instruments

Many of the songs suggest how children might use instruments. Giving children plenty of time and space to engage and experiment with varied textures and sounds, and helping them to construct sound-makers from scratch, encourages them to develop their own musical ideas.

Instruments can also help you to lead singing sessions. Several songs in this book suggest using percussion to gain the children's attention and reinforce the beat. You may find the following instruments helpful for both encouraging instrumental play and leading singing: a small drum, a large 'gathering' drum, xylophone, bells, claves, guiro, woodblock.

Specialist advice on using instruments with young children is not given in this book; p. 64 lists a number of publications which deal with this area.

Useful props

Several songs suggest using props to help reinforce meaning and encourage the children's involvement. You may find the following items useful: a selection of puppets and soft toys, a double bed sheet or lycra sheet, a sari, a rug or similar to create an instant 'singing corner', a low table on which to lay out instruments.

Foundation stage

The songs and related activities in this book fulfil many of the criteria specified by the Qualifications and Curriculum Authority (2000) for the foundation stage six areas of learning. The symbols below represent each of the six areas. The most relevant symbols for each song are given above the music.

1. Personal, social, and emotional development

2. Communication, language, and literacy

3. Mathematical development

4. Knowledge and understanding of the world

5. Physical development

6. Creative development

▦ Singing with young children

Your voice

Voiceplay assumes you will use your voice as a starting point. Many of us feel shy about singing out in front of others, and even the most confident of musicians and Early Years workers are sometimes concerned about singing 'well enough'. What is important is that yours is a voice that the children know, or get to know, as you and they become more familiar with the songs. Here are some ideas to help you get started:

- Listen to the CD; this is the quickest and easiest way to familiarize yourself with the songs. You can also practise by singing along!
- Discuss with others any singing activity you are planning for the children. This will help you focus on what's involved.
- The first time you try out a new song, try it with people you know and with whom you feel comfortable. Encourage them to join in with you. This will help your confidence.

Taking care of your voice is essential. Maintaining a quiet, strong voice rather than a high-pitched, loud one will encourage children's attentive listening. Drink plenty of water to avoid dryness and, if you are unwell with a sore throat, ask other colleagues to help you with singing.

Before starting to lead a song, take a deep breath and then exhale slowly. Relax your shoulders and smile. Think about the note that you are going to start on, and have a go. Make sure it is comfortable for you to sing—not too high, not too low.

Be clear with the children about when to listen and when to sing, and sing the song through to them at least once before expecting them to join in. If you want them to sing with you, give them their starting pitch by singing 'Ready, let's go'. Try to make sure you sing this in time with the opening of the song so that the children know when exactly to join in. Listen to the CD for help with how to do this.

Using signals to lead children in singing can be very helpful. Use your hands and arms to show pitch direction, perhaps moving your hands upwards as the pitch rises, and downwards as the pitch falls. Establish a range of hand gestures to indicate changes in dynamics or speed. For example, hands coming close together might mean getting quieter, while hands moving gradually apart might show a gradual increase in volume.

Bear in mind that children with special educational needs may need additional support from other children and adults about when to join in singing, and in following instructions like making a circle and choosing partners.

Children's voices

Singing with young children is essentially about listening to them, watching them, and relating with them through using voices expressively. It is about joining in with their spontaneous voice play and providing opportunities for extending their ideas. In these ways, singing and making music can become everyday activities.

Listen carefully to children's voices when you are leading a song. There may be several children within any group who are not matching your pitch. Listen as they get used to how a tune moves up and down. Their voices may be following the shape of the tune, but not necessarily at the same pitch as yours. If so, try adjusting your starting pitch at first to match theirs. Children need time and lots of repetition of the songs to develop their singing voices.

Some children have very low-pitched voices which, if not handled with care, may not develop into singing voices. These 'growlers' (as they are sometimes called) will begin to use their singing voices if, again, you match their pitch at first. Try using a lower starting note occasionally and start with simple songs which fall within a fairly narrow pitch range and have few big leaps in the melody. Keep these singers near you to help them join in and follow the tune.

The songs in Section 3 are specifically designed to help develop young singing voices by using short phrases, echoes, and pitch matching. You may find it helpful when singing these songs to ask the children to use their 'thinking voices'. This concept refers to the way in which we need to learn to hear songs 'in our heads' to be able to sing them confidently. Encouraging children to internalize sounds in this way will help them develop their singing skills and their understanding of musical concepts.

Finally, note that young voices are often tender and should be treated with care. Do not encourage very loud singing.

▪ Acknowledgements

We would like to thank the following individuals for the various ways in which they have contributed to this book: Angiras Auro, Amanda Brosnan, Subhadra Mittal, Tina Smith, Sally Thomas of the Oxfordshire Early Years team, Megan Wilcox of the Children, Schools, and Families Service in Hertfordshire, and Susan Young.

We would also like to thank the staff and families of the following organizations: 'Music with Mum' groups, Hertfordshire; the Roundabout Centre at the Early Years Unit, Bayards Hill School, Oxford; Weston Way Nursery School, Baldock.

Thanks are also due to the Oxford Peers Early Education Partnership leaders who tried out our ideas and to Tallulah Horton for inspiring 'Lula's lullaby'.

Special thanks to both of our families for their patience and understanding: David Bance, all at 'Bancey Castle', and Simon Street.

ALISON STREET & LINDA BANCE
Oxford, January 2006

Voice play

The breathing and voice sound activities in this section help children get ready for singing. Track 1 on the CD gives examples of the voice sounds they might make. Try to make voice play a regular part of singing sessions and give the children time to listen to each other as they try out voice sounds. The voice play song 'Copy kitten' on p. 12 provides an opportunity to build on the ideas in this section.

Before you start, have the children positioned so that you can see all of their faces, and they can easily see you.

1. Stretch and relax

This is a useful way to warm up the body and get ready to control breath.

- Ask the children to stretch and then relax their upper bodies, including arms, shoulders, and necks.

2. Breathing activities

The following activities can help children become more aware of breathing and breath control and help them to sing more freely. Take these gently; make sure that children don't get light-headed or dizzy by holding their breath for too long or taking too long to exhale.

- Ask the children to imagine that their insides are like an empty bottle. When they breathe in, keeping their shoulders down, the 'bottle' fills up with air from the bottom upwards. When the bottle is full, the lid is screwed on and the air held in.
- Now suggest that the bottle is shaken up and that the lid is partially unscrewed, quietly letting out air. Encourage the children to exhale gently by making a hissing sound.
- Ask the children to breathe in again, still imagining that their lungs are like a bottle filling with air. This time, suggest that the lid is taken off completely, so that all of the air gushes out as fast as it can. Encourage the children to 'huff' or 'whish' out all of the air in their lungs.
- Try the hissing exercise again, this time asking the children to try and alternate between exhaling and holding their breath by repeatedly hissing and stopping until they've let out all of their air. Try using hand signals to indicate when they should hiss and when they should stop.

3. Long and short sounds

These activities help to get the facial muscles moving and to develop breath control.

- Ask the children to poke out and wiggle their tongues. Suggest that they try and make voice sounds at the same time.
- Encourage the children to make lots of long sounds, for example *ssh, ss, mm, ll, ff, ch* (as in 'loch'), *rr* (like a cat purring).
- Ask the children to try making long sounds that change when they alter the shape of their mouths, such as *ee, oh, oo, ah, eh*. Ask them to listen to how these sounds change when they make funny mouth faces, such as 'wide-mouthed frogs' and fish opening and shutting their mouths.

- Ask the children to contribute their own long sound ideas; listen, and then invite everyone to join in.
- Ask the children to give ideas for short, explosive sounds that burst from the mouth, for example *t, k, b, p, tch, f*.
- Try making a soundscape combining long and short voice sounds.

4. Sliding sounds

These ideas help open up the throat and the airways.

- Ask the children to slide their voices up and down in pitch, like a siren.
- Choose an open sound, like *ah*, and encourage the children to slide and swoop freely with their voices.

5. Humming sounds

These help get the vocal cords and face resonating.

- Ask the children to hum with their eyes shut and feel with their fingertips their voices vibrating in their throats. Encourage them to change pitch so that they can feel the vibrations change as they hum higher and lower.

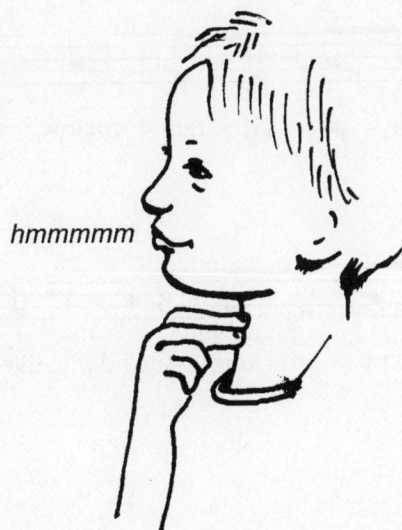

hmmmmm

Copy kitten: a voice play song

RESOURCES ▶ CD tracks 1 (voice play ideas) and 2 (song) ▶ Children's book

☐ Choose this song

- To explore voice play, using the sounds suggested on pp. 10–11 and on the CD.

☐ Get ready

- Have the children grouped in front of you.

☐ Sing this song

- Sing through the song while the children listen.
- Repeat, encouraging them to join in.
- At the end of the song, ask one child to make up a sound with their voice.
- Everybody copies the sound.

☐ Ideas

Listening and creativity

1. Repeat the song. Each time you come to the end, ask a child for a new voice play sound for everyone to copy.
2. Encourage the children to vary the sounds they make up by changing the timbre, e.g. try spiky sounds, then smooth and gentle sounds.
3. Try changing the dynamics, e.g. make the sounds louder or quieter.
4. Try altering the pitch, e.g. make the sounds higher or lower.

Linda Bance

At a steady pace

Co - py kit - ten, co - py kit - ten, miaow, miaow, hiss!

Co - py kit - ten, co - py kit - ten, sounds like this! ... *tch, tch,* etc.

Section 1

Songs to Help Things Happen

1 Sit by me

RESOURCES ▶ CD track 3 ▶ Children's book

☐ Choose this song

- To gather people together.
- To signal the start of a singing or music time.
- To allow children to join in when they're ready.

☐ Get ready

- Place yourself where there is room for others to join you, e.g. on the carpet.
- Have props or instruments to hand.
- Think of actions the children can join in with as they gather to you.
- Adapt the words of the song to suit your situation, e.g. 'if you want to clap your hands', 'if you want to play a drum'.

☐ Sing this song

- Sing the song through as many times as it takes to gather the children together.
- Encourage the children to join in with singing and the actions as they gather.

☐ Ideas

Listening and movement

1. In a larger space, change the words of the song to encourage the children to use bigger movements, e.g. 'if you want to swing your arms, swing with me'.
2. Repeat Idea 1, but this time play a drum to help support your singing, the beat, and the movement.

1 Sit by me

Melody: London Bridge
Words: Alison Street

Happily

1. If you want to sing a song, sing a song, sing a song.
2. If you want to play a drum, play a drum, play a drum.

If you want to sing a song, sit by me.____
If you want to play a drum, sit by me.____

2 Together now

RESOURCES ▶ CD track 4

☐ Choose this song

- To gather people together.
- To mark the start of a singing session or familiar routine.
- To involve everyone in getting a task done.
- To help children to listen to instructions, and to join in when ready.

☐ Get ready

- Decide what instructions you want to give.
- Make sure they fit into the rhythm of the song.

☐ Sing this song

- Keep repeating the song until the children are joining in with singing and the task is done.

☐ Ideas

Creating new actions

1. (a) Ask the children to suggest actions to help keep a steady beat, such as clapping, nodding, tapping, swaying, rocking.
    (b) All sing and repeat verse 1, using a different action with each repeat.

Listening to different timbres

2. (a) Choose an instrument or sound-maker with which to accompany the song.
    (b) Sing through the song, playing the instrument, while the children listen.
    (c) Encourage the children to find words to describe the instrument's timbre, e.g. smooth, rough, ghostly, etc.
    (d) Repeat the song, playing the instrument, this time with the children joining in.
    (e) Repeat the steps above with a different instrument. Try and choose one with a contrasting timbre.

2 Together now

Alison Street

Brightly

1. It's time to sing a song, it's time to do our mus - ic, with
2. It's time to ti - dy up, to put a - way the toys now. It's

you and me and all of us to - geth - er now.
time to put them in their box to - geth - er now.

3 Think of someone

RESOURCES ▶ CD track 5

Choose this song

- To help children feel valued.
- To introduce new names and remind of known ones.
- To reflect on feelings about being part of a group.

Get ready

- Have the children grouped in front of you.
- Start with a spoken guessing game. Think of someone in the room and describe something about them. Perhaps they came for the first time today, or maybe it's their birthday? Ask the children to guess who you are thinking about.

Sing this song

- Sing through the song while the children listen.
- Repeat, encouraging them to join in.
- Sing names clearly so that everyone can get to know them.

Ideas

Communicating feelings

1. (a) Find words to describe feelings through using a puppet. Maybe the puppet is feeling shy, worried, or angry?
   (b) Model how the puppet might sing 'hello'. Volume, timbre, and pitch can all help express its mood.
   (c) Ask the children to choose how they'd like the puppet to sound and to try and demonstrate its 'voice', e.g. if they want the puppet to sound angry, they might use growly sounds.

Listening and pitch matching

2. (a) Decide on a name for the puppet.
   (b) Sing from † to the end only. The puppet sings 'hello, everyone' and the children sing 'hello' back, using the puppet's name.
   (c) Repeat, this time with the puppet singing 'hello' to one child at a time. Encourage the named child to sing back to the puppet on their own.

Note: In Idea 2(c), some children may find it difficult to match your pitch. If so, start off by altering your pitch to match theirs.

3 Think of someone

Alison Street

Thoughtfully

Think of some-one sit-ting here to-day.   We want her to know that we

know her name.   Hel - lo *Aish - a!** Hel - lo *Aish - a!*

*Insert name as required.

4 What shall I find?

RESOURCES ▶ CD track 6 ▶ Children's book

☐ Choose this song

- To encourage sharing and acceptance of others' ideas.
- To help develop imaginative movement and expression.
- To play with rhythm patterns.

☐ Get ready

- Think how you might change the words of this song to suit the day or time of year, e.g. to help celebrate festivals such as Christmas or Eid.
- Make a circle holding hands with one child in the middle.

☐ Sing this song

- Sing through the song, all walking round in the circle, while the children listen.
- Repeat, encouraging them to join in with the singing.
- When you reach the end of verse 1, the child in the middle chooses an idea for a present and tells everyone.
- Sing verse 2, all doing actions which relate to the suggested present.

☐ Ideas

Playing with rhythms

1. (a) Place a bag of 'treasure' (toys) in the middle of the circle and walk round, all singing. At the end of verse 1, one child chooses a treasure.
   (b) This child then chants and claps a rhythm pattern to go with the name or the nature of the chosen treasure, e.g. if it's a skipping rope, the child may choose to chant 'skip and skip'.
   (c) Everyone then chants and claps the rhythm together before returning to verse 1.
   (d) Encourage the children to find different ways of showing the rhythm, e.g. clapping, stamping, slapping thighs, pointing.

Playing with instruments

2. (a) Place a selection of instruments in the centre of the circle, making sure that there is one for each child.
   (b) Walk round in the circle, all singing verse 1. At the end of verse 1, one child chooses an instrument and plays freely, in their own time, while everyone else listens.
   (c) Ask the child to show when they've finished their performance, e.g. by bowing or by standing very still. Encourage everyone else to show their appreciation by clapping.
   (d) After the performance, all choose an instrument to play while singing verse 2.

4 What shall I find?

Melody: Drunken sailor
Words: Linda Bance

With excitement

1. What shall I find in my birth - day pre - sent?
2. Let's all___ play with my birth - day pre - sent,

What shall I find in my birth - day pre - sent? What shall I find in my
let's all___ play with my birth - day pre - sent, let's all___ play with my

birth - day pre - sent? Ear - ly in the morn - ing.
birth - day pre - sent, ear - ly in the morn - ing.

5 Goodbye

RESOURCES ▶ CD track 7

☐ Choose this song

- To mark the end of a singing session.
- To say goodbye.
- To help develop social awareness.

☐ Get ready

- Make a circle with the children, sitting down on the floor and holding hands.

☐ Sing this song

- Sing through the song, swaying gently, while the children listen.
- After you've sung through the song once, encourage the children to join in with singing and swaying.

☐ Ideas

Using a song flexibly

1. Use this song in different situations, e.g. in the playground, or by the coat pegs when the children are getting ready to leave.
2. Ask the children to suggest other situations for singing this song, e.g. to say goodbye to a parent or carer when they go to work, or to another adult or friend who's been to visit.

Communicating in new ways

3. (a) Try finding other ways to sing this song, e.g. just humming and waving.
   (b) Ask the children, their parents or carers, and friends for the word 'goodbye' in other languages; see how many different 'goodbyes' you can collect and sing.

Melody: Trad. American
Words: Linda Bance

It's time to say_ good - bye,_ it's time to say_ good - bye,_ good-

- bye, good-bye, good - bye, good-bye, it's time to say good - bye._

Songs with Movement

6 Walk and stop!

RESOURCES ▶ CD track 8

☐ Choose this song

- To help physical development.
- To help develop listening skills.
- To help reinforce a steady beat.

☐ Get ready

- Listen to the CD for guidance on how to sing this song and for how long to pause after singing 'stop!'.
- In a large space, ask the children to find their own spot, not touching anyone.
- Explain that they will need to listen to you to know which movement to do, e.g. to walk, glide, or jump.
- Explain that they should move when you are singing, and stop moving when you sing 'stop!'.
- Have a drum and beater ready.

☐ Sing this song

- Lead this song by singing, walking, and beating the drum.
- Encourage the children to walk around the space, following their own paths, as you sing.
- After you sing 'stop!', stay still, and allow the children time to stop moving.
- Once all of the children are still, continue with the song, encouraging them to join in singing, until everyone is familiar with the pattern.

☐ Ideas

Exploring movement

1. Encourage the children to try other movements, such as creeping or rolling, and adjust the speed of your singing and drum playing as necessary to fit the children's pace.

Exploring dynamics through movement

2. (a) Talk about weight with the children and let them explore ways of moving, e.g. lightly, on their toes, or heavily, stamping their feet.
   (b) Help show the difference between light and heavy movements by playing the drum more gently for light movements, and more strongly for heavier movements.

6 Walk and stop!

Trad. American

Jazzy

Oh well, you walk, and you walk, and you walk, and you stop!

Oh well, you walk, and you walk, and you walk, and you stop!

7 Barney Bear

RESOURCES ▶ CD track 9 ▶ Children's book ▶ Piano accomp. p. 62

☐ Choose this song

- To help develop social awareness.
- To help develop awareness of the beat.

☐ Get ready

- In a large space, ask the children to find their own spot, not touching anyone.
- Have a drum and beater ready.

☐ Sing this song

- Sing through the song, playing a steady walking beat on the drum in part 1 and a faster beat in part 2.
- As you sing part 1, ask the children to walk around the space, following their own paths.
- At the end of part 1, encourage each child to find a partner. Everyone then stands still, holding their partner's hands, listening for the start of part 2.
- In part 2, the rhythm changes and the beat becomes faster; encourage the children to dance with their partners as you play and sing.
- Repeat the song, encouraging the children to join in singing and to choose a new partner each time you get to the end of part 1.

☐ Ideas

Taking turns to move and to play instruments

1. (a) Divide the children into two groups: one for movement, and one for playing instruments such as chime bars, scrapers, etc.
   (b) Encourage the instrumental group to accompany part 1 by playing at a walking pace. It will help them to keep a steady beat if they chant 'walking, walking' as they play. The CD shows how to do this.
   (c) Encourage faster playing for part 2 when the movement group is dancing. Both groups should try to stop together at the end of the song.
   (d) Swap over the two groups so that all children have the chance to play instruments and to move.

Moving imaginatively

2. Ask the children to suggest and show other movements for Barney, such as jumping, rolling, and gliding. Encourage them to try these out, changing the words in the song, and their singing voices, to match the movement.

Note: Don't worry if the children are not able to stick to a steady beat in part 2; it's not essential. The musical aims are to try to establish a walking beat in part 1, to make a change of speed in part 2, and to stop together at the end.

7 Barney Bear

Part 1
At a walking pace

C   C   G   C

Bar - ney Bear is walk - ing, walk - ing, walk - ing.

5   C   C   G   C

Bar - ney Bear is walk - ing, walk - ing to the park.

Part 2
Faster

9   C   F   C   C   F   G

Bar - ney Bear has found a friend, Bar - ney Bear has found a friend,

13   Am   G   F   C   C   G   C

Bar - ney Bear has found a friend, go - ing to the park.

© Oxford University Press 2006

7. Barney Bear   **27**

8 Two teddies on a trampoline

RESOURCES ▶ CD track 10

☐ Choose this song

- To help with confidence and turn taking.
- To help develop number awareness.
- To help reinforce a steady beat.

☐ Get ready

- Make a circle with two children in the middle.

☐ Sing this song

- Sing this song with the children clapping or slapping knees to the beat while the two 'teddies' perform their own actions in the middle of the circle.
- At the end of the song, call out the names of the two children in the middle to show them that it's time for two others in the circle to have a go.
- Repeat the song until everyone has had a turn in the middle, encouraging the children to join in with singing as well as clapping and doing the actions.

☐ Ideas

Counting

1. If your group is big enough, sing the song with numbers going upwards and downwards. After each verse, two more children join the two already in the middle until it's time to start taking away the 'teddies', two by two.
2. (a) The children sit in a circle, holding the edge of a large, stretched bed or lycra sheet.
   (b) All sing through the song, bouncing teddy bears up and down on the sheet. The bears can be added or subtracted two at a time, as well as bounced off the sheet.

Taking turns and playing instruments

3. (a) All of the children sit in a circle. Divide them into two groups; group 1 sings through the song while the children in group 2 play instruments such as drums or chimes on the beat. It will help group 2 establish a steady beat if they chant 'boing, boing' as they play.
   (b) Swap over the groups so that everyone has a turn at singing and playing.

8 Two teddies on a trampoline

With bounce!

Linda Bance

D .... D .... D .... D ...... A

Two   ted-dies on   a   tram - po - line,   boing, boing,   boing, boing!

D .... D .... D ... A .... D

Two   ted-dies on   a   tram - po - line,   boing, boing,   boing!

9 Sally go round the sun

RESOURCES ▶ CD track 11 ▶ Children's book

☐ Choose this song

- To help creative development.
- To help develop listening skills.
- To help physical development.

☐ Get ready

- Make a circle, standing up and holding hands.

☐ Sing this song

- Sing through the song while the children listen and walk round in the circle.
- When you say 'Boom!', everyone kicks one leg up in the air.
- Repeat the song, walking round in the opposite direction and kicking again on 'Boom!'.
- Repeat, encouraging the children to join in with the singing as well as moving.

☐ Ideas

Listening and movement

1. (a) Make three large pictures or models, one each of the sun, the moon, and a chimney pot.
   (b) Ask the children to sit on the floor in a large circle, and place the pictures/models on the floor within the circle.
   (c) While everyone sings, one child travels from their place in the circle around the 'sun', the 'moon', and the 'chimney pot'.
   (d) On 'Boom!', the child plops back into their place in the circle.

Moving imaginatively

2. Ask the children to suggest other movement ideas, such as jumping, rolling, and gliding, and encourage them to try these out, adapting both their singing style and the words to suit their movements.

Using a song flexibly

3. Adapt the words of the song to suit other occasions, and ask the children to think of relevant objects to move around, e.g. Sally could go round a cat, a star, and a witch's hat 'on Halloween afternoon'.

Note: Although a child may be jumping or hopping very fast, they may take a long time to get round each picture and back to their place in the circle in time for 'Boom!'. Try to adjust your singing to match the pace of the child's movement.

9 Sally go round the sun

Trad. English

Brightly

D | D | G | D

Sal - ly go round the sun, Sal - ly go round the moon,

A | D | A | D — Spoken

Sal - ly go round the chim - ney pot on a Thurs - day af - ter - noon. *Boom!*

Songs to Help Singing Voices

10 On a log

RESOURCES ▶ CD track 12 ▶ Children's book

☐ Choose this song

- To help language development.
- To help pitch matching.
- To help develop rhythmic skills.

☐ Get ready

- Have the children grouped in front of you.

☐ Sing this song

- Sing through the song at a steady pace, asking the children to join in with 'Glumf! Glumf! Glumf! Glumf!'.
- Repeat, encouraging the children to join in with the whole verse.

☐ Ideas

Playing with instruments and rhythm

1. (a) Have a selection of instruments to hand.
    (b) Divide the children into two groups. Group 1 sings and group 2 plays instruments.
    (c) Ask all of the children to choose which of the instruments and their sounds should represent each animal.
    (d) Group 1 sings through the song but stops at * to allow group 2 to play the animal sounds.
    (e) Swap over the two groups and repeat steps (c) and (d) so that all of the children have the chance to sing, and to choose and play instruments.

Creating new ideas

2. Encourage the children to have a go at making up new verses with other animals and their sounds.
3. Help the children to remember or to think of imaginary beasts or animals they've met in stories or in films, and to create sounds to go with them.

Note: You may find it particularly useful to re-read the 'Singing with young children' section on p. 8 before trying songs 10–13.

10 On a log

Trad. American
vv. 2 & 3: words by Alison Street

At a steady pace

1. On a log, Mis - ter Frog, sang his song the
2. In a pen, Mis - sus Hen, clucked a - round and
3. In a hole, Mis - ter Mole, curled up tight and

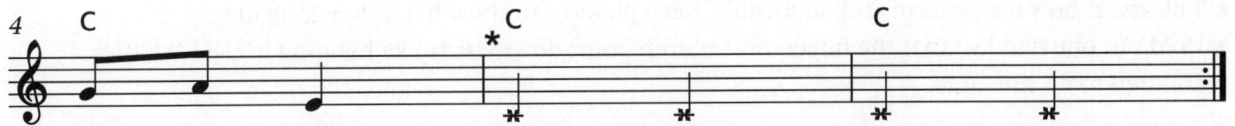

whole day long, glumf, glumf, glumf, glumf!
scratched the ground, squawk, squawk, squawk, squawk!
slept 'til night, snore, snore, snore, snore!

11 Five icicles

RESOURCES ▸ CD tracks 13 (song) and 14 (soundscape) ▸ Children's book

☐ Choose this song

- To help pitch matching.
- To help develop number awareness.
- To help creative development.
- To help coordination skills.

☐ Get ready

- Have the children grouped in front of you.
- Talk about how icicles form and, if possible, have pictures to show what they look like.
- Hold out one hand so that the fingers and thumb point downwards like hanging icicles. Ask the children to do the same.

☐ Sing this song

- Sing through the first verse steadily. At the end of the verse, speak (rather than sing) the line 'one melted—*mm!*', making a long humming sound from high to low to suggest melting ice. Listen to the CD for help with this.
- Tuck in your thumb to show that one 'icicle' has melted.
- Repeat, encouraging the children to join in with both singing and hand actions, tucking in one finger at a time as each icicle melts.

☐ Ideas

Playing instruments imaginatively

1. (a) Talk about 'cold' sounds using words like 'shivering' and 'freezing'.
   (b) Encourage the children to make up 'shivering' music with instruments like shakers and bells.
   (c) Talk about 'melting' sounds, using words like 'dripping' and 'trickling'.
   (d) Encourage the children to make up 'melting' music with instruments such as chime bars, xylophones, and woodblocks.

Creating a soundscape using breath and body sounds

2. (a) All together, try doing some of the breathing and voice play ideas on pp. 10–11.
   (b) Make up a 'wintry' soundscape using voice sounds, e.g. whispering and sighing, and body percussion, e.g. rubbing hands together and stamping feet. Track 14 on the CD provides an example.

11 Five icicles

Linda Bance

Wintry

Five*   i - ci - cles,   five   i - ci - cles,

five   i - ci - cles   hang-ing   a - round.

Spoken

One melted—*mm!*

*Reduce each time you sing through the song until there are no icicles left.

12 Seer moonday goday paer (Head and shoulders)

RESOURCES ▶ CD track 15 ▶ Piano accomp. p. 62

☐ Choose this song

- To help pitch matching.
- To help coordination skills.
- To help language skills.
- To help awareness of different languages.

☐ Get ready

- Listen to the CD for guidance on how to pronounce the Punjabi words. Try to remember the Punjabi version and start with this.
- Have the children sitting in a circle on the floor with their legs stretched out in front of them.
- Explain that the words of the song are about different parts of the body.

☐ Sing this song

- Sing through the first verse (Punjabi version) pronouncing the words clearly and pointing to the relevant parts of the body.
- Encourage the children to join in, first with singing and clapping on the 'Clap, clap, clap, clap, clap' sections, and then with all of the words.
- Sing through the English version, encouraging the children to point at their heads, shoulders, etc., and then repeat the Punjabi version with the children continuing to point at the relevant parts of their bodies.

☐ Ideas

Communicating in different languages

1. Ask the children, their parents, and friends for the words in other languages. See how many different versions you can collect and sing.
2. (a) If possible, try a multilingual version of the song. Ask the children to take it in turns to sing in their chosen language.
    (b) The other children should listen and join in where possible.
    (c) Everyone should clap on the 'Clap, clap, clap, clap, clap' sections.

12 Seer moonday goday paer (Head and shoulders)

Trad. English
v. 2 Punjabi

At a steady pace

1. Seer___ moon-day go - day paer, go - day paer, go - day paer.
2. Head and should-ers, knees and toes, knees and toes, knees and toes.

Seer___ moon-day go - day paer, clap, clap, clap, clap, clap!
Head and should-ers, knees and toes,

*Naa - lay akh,___ naa - lay kan, naa - lay moo, naa - lay nak.
Eyes and ears and mouth and nose, mouth and nose, mouth and nose.

Seer___ moon-day go - day paer, clap, clap, clap, clap, clap!
Head and should-ers, knees and toes,

*When singing line 3 of the Punjabi version, actions are as follows:

naalay akh—point to eyes
naalay kan—point to ears
naalay moo—point to mouth
naalay nak—point to nose

13 Where is Bear?

RESOURCES ▶ CD track 16

☐ Choose this song

- To help pitch matching.
- To help develop listening skills.
- To help develop imagination.

☐ Get ready

- Have the children grouped in front of you.
- Explain that this is a song about echoes. Talk about what an echo is, and how it might sound.

☐ Sing this song

- Sing phrase 1 ('Bear on the mountain') and ask the children to 'be the echo' and sing it back to you.
- Sing through the whole song in this fashion. Use a hand signal to show the children when to sing each echo.
- At the end of the song, ask one child to choose a new hiding place for Bear, e.g. 'Bear in the kitchen'.
- Sing the song again using the child's idea. At the end, ask a different child for another hiding place, and repeat the song.

☐ Ideas

Taking turns and playing with dynamics

1. (a) Divide the children into two groups. Group 1 sings phrases 1–4, and group 2 sings each echo.
   (b) Once both groups can sing their parts with confidence, try different dynamics, e.g. ask group 1 to sing their phrases more quietly, and group 2 to sing the echoes more quietly still.
   (c) Swap the groups so that everyone has a turn at singing the echoes.
   (d) Try other ways of changing the dynamics, e.g. getting gradually louder or quieter.

Listening

2. (a) Make a 'microphone' out of a cardboard tube with a ping-pong ball taped to one end, or improvise with an object that looks like a microphone.
   (b) Explain to the children that when you hold the microphone up, they are to sing out loud. When the microphone disappears behind your back, they should stop singing out loud but try and carry on singing the song in their heads, e.g. using their 'thinking voices'.
   (c) Sing through the song, holding the microphone up and all singing aloud in phrases 1–4. Hold the microphone behind your back during the echo sections and stop singing. You may need to remind the children not to sing.
   (d) Experiment with holding up and hiding the microphone in other parts of the song.
   (e) Let one of the children have a go at holding up/hiding the microphone while everyone else sings/is quiet.

13 Where is Bear?

Linda Bance

Steadily

Phrase 1   Echo 1   Phrase 2

1. Bear on the mount - ain, Bear on the mount - ain, Hel - lo Bear,
2. Bear in the bed - room, Bear in the bed - room, Hel - lo Bear,
3. Bear on the so - fa, Bear on the so - fa, Hel - lo Bear,

Echo 2   Phrase 3   Echo 3

Hel - lo Bear. Bear on the mount - ain, Bear on the mount - ain.
Hel - lo Bear. Bear in the bed - room, Bear in the bed - room.
Hel - lo Bear. Bear on the so - fa, Bear on the so - fa.

Phrase 4   Echo 4

I know you're there, I won - der where?
I know you're there, I won - der where?
I know you're there, I won - der where?

Section 4

Songs for Play

14 Roll a ball

RESOURCES ▶ CD track 17

☐ Choose this song

- To help pitch matching.
- To help develop social awareness.
- To help coordination skills.

☐ Get ready

- All sit in a circle on the floor with space enough for a ball to be rolled across from one child in the circle to another.
- Have a large, soft ball ready to hand.
- Choose a child's name to sing out.

☐ Sing this song

- Sing the song through while the children listen. As you sing the name of your chosen child (at the end of line 2), roll the ball to them.
- Encourage the child to keep hold of the ball until the last line of the song, and then to roll it back to you.
- Repeat the song, rolling the ball to a different child and encouraging the children to join in with singing.

☐ Ideas

Encouraging individual singing skills

1. (a) Sing lines 1 and 2 only, rolling the ball to a child as you sing their name. Ask that child to repeat the first two lines and to choose someone else to roll the ball to.
   (b) Continue to repeat lines 1 and 2 in this way, until all of the children have had a chance to roll the ball and to sing.

Playing with dynamics

2. Vary the dynamics; try the song quieter then louder, and ask the children for their ideas.

Making larger movements

3. All standing up, make a bigger circle, and sing the song again either rolling or bouncing the ball.

14 Roll a ball

Linda Bance

Smoothly

Roll a ball, roll a ball,

roll a ball to Jo - dy.*

Jo - dy has got the ball,

roll it back to me.

*Insert name as required.

15 Round, round, round

RESOURCES ▶ CD track 18

☐ Choose this song

- To encourage play.
- To help creative development.
- To help develop knowledge and understanding of the world.

☐ Get ready

- Either join the children where they are playing, or have them grouped in front of you.
- Ask the children to check there is enough space for them to stretch their arms out in front of them without touching anyone else.
- Have a toy train and a bowl of play-dough to hand.

☐ Sing this song

- Sing through verse 1 steadily while the children listen. Throughout, move each arm in turn as if drawing large circles in front of you.
- Repeat, encouraging the children to join in with both singing and arm movements.
- For verses 2 and 3, use the toy train and play-dough as visual aids.

☐ Ideas

Moving imaginatively

1. (a) In a large space, give the children streamers and ask them to find their own spot, not touching anyone else.
   (b) Sing through verse 1, making circles above, beside, or behind you with your streamer.
   (c) Encourage the children to join in with singing and making circles with their streamers in the same way.
2. (a) In a large space, ask the children to make themselves into a 'train', with an 'engine' at the front and 'trucks' behind.
   (b) The engine sings through verse 2 as written while the trucks chant 'chug', in their own time, throughout.
   (c) Everyone follows each other around the space, singing and making 'wheel' movements with their arms by their sides.
   (d) Swap the children over so that everyone has a turn at being the engine and the trucks.

15 Round, round, round

Expressively

Alison Street

1. Make a cir - cle in the air, round, round, round.
2. Run the eng - ine down the line, chug, chug, chug.
3. Stir the play-dough, roll it out, splat, splat, splat!

Like a wheel__ spin - ning there, round, round, round.
Pull the coach a - long be - hind, chug, chug, chug.
Mix it up and tip it out, splat, splat, splat!

16 Under the cover

RESOURCES ▶ CD track 19 ▶ Children's book

☐ Choose this song

- To encourage children to express feelings.
- To help creative development.

☐ Get ready

- Have the children sitting in a circle on the floor, with a blanket in the middle.
- Introduce the song by hiding a puppet under the blanket and talk about how it might be feeling, e.g. shy, angry, etc.
- Bring the puppet out from beneath the blanket and make it act out how it feels.

☐ Sing this song

- Sing through part 1 of the song, hiding the puppet under the blanket. When you get to part 2, bring the puppet out to show how it is feeling. Try to sing part 2 in a way which reflects the puppet's emotion.
- Ask a child to hide under the blanket. Sing through part 1, encouraging all of the children to join in.
- Stop singing at the end of part 1 and ask the child to come out from beneath the blanket. Ask them to show how they are feeling, e.g. happy, frightened, etc.
- All together, try to sing part 2 in a way which expresses the child's emotion, e.g. if the child is angry, everyone might sing in a growly voice.

☐ Ideas

Exploring facial expressions

1. (a) Talk with the children about faces, the colour of eyes, skin, and hair, and how faces help to show what we feel.
   (b) Play 'Funny faces' (a bit like 'Simon says . . .').
   (c) Ask the children to cover their faces with their hands.
   (d) Everyone counts '1, 2, 3, . . .' and waits for you to suggest a feeling, e.g. sad.
   (e) Everyone takes away their hands and tries to make a sad face.
   (f) Repeat using other emotions.
   (g) If you say 'Funny face' only (with no counting), everyone has to pull a funny face.

Using the whole body to express feelings

2. When singing the song, encourage the children to use their bodies and faces (in addition to their voices) to express their emotions, e.g. if the chosen feeling is 'excited', everyone might sing in squeaky voices, smile, and jump up and down.

Note: Some children may find it easier to express their emotions through using a puppet or favourite teddy.

16 Under the cover

Expressively

Part 1

Linda Bance

I am hid - ing un-der the cov - er, un-der the cov - er, un-der the cov - er.

I am hid - ing un-der the cov - er, guess how I will be?

Part 2

I'll be ve-ry, ve-ry hap-py,* ve-ry, ve-ry hap-py, that's how I will be.

*Change as required.

17 Lula's lullaby

RESOURCES ▶ CD track 20 ▶ Children's book

☐ Choose this song

- To encourage social development and role play.
- To explore emotions.
- To help children to relax.

☐ Get ready

- Either join the children where they are playing, or have them grouped in front of you.
- Give each of them a doll or soft toy to hold.
- Talk with the children about why babies cry, about putting babies to bed when they are tired, and about singing them a lullaby to soothe them.

☐ Sing this song

- Sing through the lullaby, rocking a doll or soft toy and swaying.
- Sing through again, encouraging the children to join in with singing, rocking their soft toy, and swaying with the music.

☐ Ideas

Playing with 'babies'

1. (a) Ask the children to give their toys a name.
   (b) Sing through the song several times so that the children can rock and sing to their own toys, singing the name of their 'baby' in bar 3, e.g. 'My Bobby sleep-a-by'.
2. Encourage a few children to move gently around the room with their 'babies' while others sing the lullaby for them.
3. (a) Ask the children about a baby they know, e.g. a sibling, and talk about how babies show what they need, what makes them smile, and what they like to play with.
   (b) Talk about ways of comforting a crying baby.
   (c) Find out about rhymes, songs, or games they have heard people use with babies, e.g. 'Round and round the garden', 'Peep-bo'.
   (d) If possible, try doing some of these songs and rhymes together, and talk about which ones sound good for playing with a baby and which sound good for soothing a baby.

17 Lula's lullaby

For Tallulah

Alison Street

Soothingly

1. Rock - a - by, lull - a - by, my ba - by sleep - a - by.
2. Rock - a - by, lull - a - by, why do you cry - a - by?

Stars in the sky - a - by, twin - kle good - night.
I love you so, and I kiss you good - night.

Songs that Tell Stories

18 Gingerbread Man

RESOURCES ► CD track 21 ► Children's book

☐ Choose this song

- To help develop listening skills.
- To help children understand about sequence in a story.
- To help language development.
- To help develop rhythmic skills.

☐ Get ready

- Have the children gathered in front of you.
- Read or tell the story of the 'Gingerbread Man'.

☐ Sing this song

- Begin the story again and sing the song each time the Gingerbread Man challenges a character to run after him. Listen to the CD for help with this.
- Repeat the story and encourage the children to join in singing with you at the right times.

☐ Ideas

Playing with rhythm

1. (a) Encourage the children to sing and repeat the first three words of the song, 'run, run, run . . .' in the same rhythm as in the song.
   (b) Once they're confident doing this, ask them to clap their hands on each 'run'.
   (c) Ask the children to keep clapping the rhythm but stop singing.
   (d) Once all the children can clap the rhythm, divide them into two groups. Group 1 sings through the song while group 2 claps the 'run, run, run' rhythm pattern throughout.
   (e) Try using instruments such as drums or scrapers to play the 'run, run, run' pattern instead of clapping.
   (f) Swap over the two groups so that everyone has a turn at singing and clapping/playing.
   (g) Repeat steps (a) to (f) using the words and rhythm pattern 'Little old woman and little old man'.
2. (a) Make gingerbread men puppets out of sticks and paper plates or card.
   (b) Re-tell the story with everyone singing the song and making the gingerbread men puppets bounce up and down throughout the song.

18 Gingerbread Man

Linda Bance

Rhythmically

Run, run, run, as fast as you can, you can't catch me I'm the Gin-ger-bread Man.

Lit-tle old wo-man and lit-tle old man, you can't catch me I'm the Gin-ger-bread Man!

19 I have a puppy

RESOURCES ▶ CD track 22

☐ Choose this song

- To help develop imagination.
- To help develop rhythmic skills.
- To help language development.

☐ Get ready

- Have the children gathered around you.
- Have a soft toy dog and cat to hand.
- Talk about the different sounds these two animals might make.

☐ Sing this song

- Sing through the first verse and first chorus, wagging the dog's tail in the chorus.
- Repeat the chorus, encouraging the children to join in singing 'Waggle, waggle' etc. and with the 'woof!'.
- Repeat the first verse, encouraging the children to join in with the singing.
- Sing through the rest of the song, encouraging the children to join in with both the singing and with making the animal noises.

☐ Ideas

Playing with sounds

1. (a) Once the song is familiar, ask children to suggest other names for the puppy starting with 'p', or for the cat, starting with 'c'.
   (b) Encourage the children to suggest different animals for the song and names to go with them, e.g. 'I have a mouse called Monty'.
   (c) Ask the children to suggest and demonstrate voice/body sounds for the animals.
   (d) All sing the children's versions of the song.

Moving imaginatively

2. In a large space, encourage the children to do the actions of the dog, cat, fish, and other animals as they sing through the song.

19 I have a puppy

Melody: Keep that wheel a-turning
Words: Linda Bance

Playfully

Verse

1. I have a pup-py called Pon - go,   I have a pup-py called Pon - go,
2. I have a cat__ called Car - los,   I have a cat__ called Car - los,
3. I have a fish__ called Fi - fi,   I have a fish__ called Fi - fi,

I have a pup-py called Pon - go,   he wags his tail all day.
I have a cat__ called Car - los,   he purrs and purrs all day.
I have a fish__ called Fi - fi,   she flips and flaps all day.

Chorus

Wag - gle, wag - gle, wag - gle, wag - gle, wag - gle, wag - gle, woof!
Purr,_____ purr,_____ purr,_____ miaow!
Flip,__ flap,__ flip,__ flap,__ flip,__ flap,__ pop!

Wag-gle, wag-gle, wag-gle, wag-gle, wag-gle, wag-gle, woof!   Wag-gle, wag-gle, wag-gle, wag-gle,
Purr,_____ purr,_____ purr,_____ miaow!   Purr,_____ purr,_____
Flip,__ flap,__ flip,__ flap,__ flip,__ flap,__ pop!   Flip,__ flap,__ flip,__ flap,__

wag - gle, wag - gle, woof!   He wags his tail all day.
purr,_____ miaow!   He purrs and purrs all day.
flip,__ flap,__ pop!   She flips and flaps all day.

20 I live in the city

RESOURCES ▶ CD track 23 ▶ Piano accomp. p. 63

☐ Choose this song

• To reflect on our needs for each other.
• To learn about valuing people in our communities.
• To reinforce a steady walking beat.

☐ Get ready

• Have the children grouped in front of you.
• Adapt the words to include the name of the nearest town/city to where the children live, e.g. 'I live in Luton, yes I do'.
• Keep the speed steady—there are a lot of words for small tongues to get round!

☐ Sing this song

• Firstly, sing right through the song while the children listen.
• Start by teaching the children the chorus, line by line, and then all try singing it right through.
• Then divide the verse into two sections, as indicated on the music.
• Ask the children to listen carefully as you sing through section 1.
• Repeat section 1 and ask the children to join in with you.
• Ask the children to listen carefully as you sing through section 2.
• Repeat section 2 and ask the children to join in with you.
• When you have worked through the whole song in this way, and the children have grasped the melody, try singing the entire way through all together.

☐ Ideas

Creating drama through role play

1. (a) With the children, make a list of the jobs and types of work which adults do, and try fitting them into the song, e.g. 'All together build this town' might become 'Work in the hospitals in this town'.
   (b) Divide the children into two groups. Group 1 sings and group 2 acts out the jobs group 1 sings about.
   (c) Swap over the groups so that everyone has a turn at singing and acting.

Playing with the beat

2. (a) Find a hard floor surface or, if possible, a large gathering drum.
   (b) All of the children kneel and beat on the floor/drum the rhythm of the words 'black hands, white hands'.
   (c) Divide the children into two groups. Group 1 sings through the song. Group 2 beats out the 'black hands, white hands' rhythm during the verse.
   (d) Swap groups so that everyone has a turn at singing and beating.
3. (a) Find a number of small wooden spoons.
   (b) Ask the children to make different coloured hand prints on paper to cut out and fasten to the spoons.
   (c) Repeat Idea 2 with the children using the decorated spoons to beat on the floor. The paper hands should dance up and down in time as the children play.

20 I live in the city

Melody: Alison Street
Words: Anon.

At a steady pace

Chorus

I live in the ci - ty,   yes I do,   I live in the ci - ty,   yes I do,

I live in the ci - ty,   yes I do,   made by hu - man hands.

Verse—section 1

Black hands, white hands,   yel-low and brown,   all to - geth - er   build this town.

Verse—section 2

Black hands, white hands, yel-low and brown,   all to-geth-er make the wheels go round.

21 The wolf's tale

RESOURCES ▶ CD track 24 ▶ Children's book ▶ Piano accomp. p. 63

☐ Choose this song

- To play with a story.
- To help with understanding other people's views.
- To explore emotions.
- To help creative development.

☐ Get ready

- Have the children grouped in front of you.
- Read or tell the story of the 'Three little pigs' with the aid of a picture book.

☐ Sing this song

- Introduce this song as an alternative version of the story.
- Sing through the whole song while the children listen.
- Encourage the children to join in with you. Start singing from the last line of the song ('I moved in . . .') and, using a hand signal, ask them to join in with the words 'And we're really, really, really, really happy'.
- When the children are able to sing this part, go back to the beginning and break the song into short sections, e.g. the first section might be 'I'm a big, bad wolf, my name is Keith'.
- Sing the sections to the children in sequence, and ask them to repeat each one after you.
- When you have worked through the whole song in this way, and the children have grasped the melody, try singing the entire way through all together.

☐ Ideas

Acting the wolf's part

1. (a) Talk about 'huffing' and 'puffing' and how this might sound. Encourage the children to experiment with using big and small breaths to make both long and short 'huffs' and 'puffs'.
   (b) Discuss how huffing and puffing might look if expressed on faces and with body gestures.
   (c) Divide the children into two groups. Group 1 sings the first half of the song (from the beginning until the line ending ' . . . new dentures'). The children in group 2 act the part of the wolf, thinking about how he might move while huffing and puffing.
   (d) Keep repeating this first half of the song over and over, swapping over the groups from time to time so that everyone has a turn at singing and acting.

Using dynamics

2. Encourage the children to try singing the first half of the song with loud voices, and the second part of the song with quieter voices.

Using different timbres

3. Ask the children to vary the sound of their voices. Encourage them to try using gruff, 'wolf-like' voices for the first half, and high, squeaky 'piglet' voices on 'And we're really, really, really, really happy'.

21 The wolf's tale

Melody: Alison Street
Words: Kaye Umansky

Huffily

I'm a big, bad wolf, my name is Keith, I'll tell you my ad-

-ven-tures. I huffed and I puffed 'til I blew out my teeth and I

had to get new den-tures. So now I can-not huff, and

now I can-not puff, I am no long-er snap-py. I moved in with the

lit-tle___ pigs, and we're real-ly, real-ly, real-ly, real-ly hap-py!___

Piano accompaniments

7 Barney Bear

Part 1
At a walking pace

Linda Bance

Bar-ney Bear is walk-ing, walk-ing, walk-ing. Bar-ney Bear is walk-ing, walk-ing to the park.

Part 2
Faster

Bar-ney Bear has found a friend, Bar-ney Bear has found a friend,

Bar-ney Bear has found a friend, go-ing to the park.

12 Seer moonday goday paer (Head and Shoulders)

Trad. English
v. 2 Punjabi

At a steady pace

1. Seer moon-day go-day paer, go-day paer, go-day paer. Seer moon-day
2. Head and should-ers, knees and toes, knees and toes, knees and toes. Head and should-ers,

go-day paer, clap, clap, clap, clap, clap! Naa-lay akh, naa-lay kan,
knees and toes, Eyes and ears and mouth and nose,

naa-lay moo, naa-lay nak. Seer moon-day go-day paer, clap, clap, clap, clap, clap!
mouth and nose, mouth and nose. Head and should-ers, knees and toes,

This page may be photocopied

20 I live in the city

Melody: Alison Street
Words anon.

Chorus
At a steady pace

I live in the ci - ty, yes I do, I live in the ci - ty, yes I do,

I live in the ci - ty, yes I do, made by hu - man hands.

Verse—section 1

Black hands, white hands, yel - low and brown, all to - geth - er build this town.

Verse—section 2

Black hands, white hands, yel - low and brown, all to - geth-er make the wheels go round.

21 The wolf's tale

Melody: Alison Street
Words: Kaye Umansky

Huffily

I'm a big, bad wolf, my name is Keith, I'll tell you my ad - ven-tures. I

huffed and I puffed 'til I blew out my teeth and I had to get new den - tures. So

now I can - not huff, and now I can - not puff, I am no long - er snap - py.

I moved in with the lit-tle___ pigs, and we're real - ly, real - ly, real - ly, real - ly hap-py!___

No. 20 may be photocopied. It is illegal to photocopy No. 21.

Piano

Reading list

Bobbie Gargrave, Helen MacGregor: *Let's Go Zudie-o: Creative Activities for Dance and Music* (A and C Black, London, 2001).

Veronicah Larkin, Louie Suthers: *What Will We Play Today? Drama, Movement and Music Games for Children Aged 0–5 Years* (Brilliant Publications, Dunstable).

Elizabeth Matterson: *This Little Puffin* (Puffin, London, 1991).

Kim Merry: *The Big, Big Multi-Cultural Music-Book 1* (Merry Publications, Sheffield).

National Youth Choir of Scotland, Lucinda Geoghegan: *Singing Games and Rhymes for Early Years* (NYCOS Publications, Glasgow, 1999).

Peers Early Education Partnership (PEEP), Alison Street: *Singing Together 2: Songs and Rhymes for Young Children* (PEEP, Oxford, 2004).

Linda Pound, Chris Harrison: *Supporting Musical Development in the Early Years* (Open University Press, 2002).

Kaye Umansky: *Three Tapping Teddies: Musical Stories and Chants for the Very Young* (A and C Black, London, 2000).

Susan Young: *Music with the Under Fours* (RoutledgeFalmer, London, 2003).

Susan Young, Joanna Glover: *Music in the Early Years* (RoutledgeFalmer, London, 1998).

CD credits

Singers/voices: Alice Atkins, David Atkins, Edward Atkins, Linda Bance, Mary Bance, Tom Bower, Jon Fletcher, Chloë Musson, Chloe Smith, Hannah Smith, Alison Street

Guitar: Linda Bance, Jon Fletcher, Alison Street
Piano: Louise Atkins, Alison Street
Viola: Jane Griffiths
Bass: Tom Bower, Colin Fletcher
Percussion/whistles: Linda Bance, Alison Street
Drums: Cameron Grote

Recorded and mixed by Jon Fletcher at the Ark-T Studio, Oxford, April 2005.
Mastered at Turan Audio, Oxford.